Design by Elizabeth Woll

Published by The C.R. Gibson Company
Made in the U.S.A.
ISBN 0-8378-9858-7
GB646

Thank You for Being You

Photographs by
Kim Anderson

Poetry by Paula Finn

THE C.R. GIBSON COMPANY, NORWALK, CONNECTICUT

One of the greatest gifts of our
    relationship
is the comfort of knowing
I can always be myself with you,
and you will accept me
for being just that.

With you,
I never have to laugh
when I feel like crying,
or be quiet
when I need to talk,
or stay calm
when I feel like getting upset,
or sound positive
when I need to complain.

The greatest comfort is the
knowledge
that when I need a friend...
I never have to be alone.

*I*n sharing our fears,
we become bolder.
In sharing our losses,
we become richer.
In sharing our mistakes,
we become wiser.

In sharing ourselves,
        we become closer.

*Our lives were meant
    to be shared.*

*I*t's so comforting to share the events
of my day with you—
the little things I know you'll find
funny,
or touching,
or interesting,
only because they happened to me.

You know when I need
your help or advice,
and when I just need
to know that you care.

*I*t's not often
that we feel safe enough
with another person
to shed our defenses,
and to risk being completely
        ourselves—
to show them they are important in
        our life,
and that we would be so much less
without them.

I need you . . .
and I trust you enough
to tell you.

*Y*ou listen to me
without judging,
you support me
without pressuring,
you appreciate me as I am
without comparing me
to what I am not.

You encourage me
in my goals and dreams,
and validate my struggles
to fulfill them ...

You are
so easy to talk to,
so easy to feel close to,
and so easy to love.

*Y*our support
has deepened my self-confidence,
your humor
has brightened my outlook,
and your encouragement
has brought me closer than ever
to my dreams.

Always,
you've been there
to listen, to understand . . .
and to help me grow.

Your support adds so much
to my life.
You share my joy
as if it were your own.
You feel my pain
and you cry with me.

Thank you for
understanding me,
accepting me,
and loving me as I am.

*I*t sounds simple
but it means so much to say
I feel comfortable with you.
I don't have to worry
about how I look to you
or sound to you
or what you're going to think
     about me
when I'm not around.
I don't have to rehearse or analyze
our conversations—
when we talk
I can relax.

I feel comfortable with you.
It sounds so simple ...
but it means so much.

You know when I want to be
    serious;
you know when I need to be playful.
When I'm with you
I am free to express my true mood.
If I'm not feeling happy,
or positive, or energetic,
I don't have to act
or pretend that I am.
You support my goals,
while accepting my faults.
You love the person I am.

Your accepting nature
has helped me to treat others
and myself, more gently.
You concentrate on my good points
while overlooking my flaws,
and you can always find
something in me to praise.

You are so thoughtful.
You give me much more than is
        expected
and you expect much less than you
        deserve.

You are strong enough
to admit your weaknesses,
brave enough to express your fears;
free enough to laugh
and human enough to cry.

*M*y life is enriched in so
many ways
by your presence,
for in you I have found the friend
I've always wanted...
and the love I'll always need.

Together
we've laughed and cried
shared sunshine and storms ...
we've celebrated carefree days,
and helped each other through
the long troubled nights.

Your support
has made my triumphs more
        meaningful,
and my losses easier to bear.

I will praise you when you win,
and share your pain if you lose…

always, I will accept you for who
        you are
and not for how much
or how little you achieve.

I will strive to bring out the best
        in you
while forgiving your faults.

I won't expect perfection
in either of us.

*I*n the tomorrows we share,
I pray that I can be
sensitive to your needs,
understanding of your concerns,
patient with your mistakes,
and comforting of your pain…
that I can give as much of myself as
you need…

and all the love that you deserve.

With you
life is exciting.
With you
I can be myself.
With you
I feel appreciated.
With you
I have fun.
With you
I am happier than
        I have ever been.
Thank you for being you.